T0102459

EVERYDAY CODING__

COMPLETING TASKS

Using Algorithms

Derek Miller

Cavendish
Square

New York

Published in 2018 by Cavendish Square Publishing, LLC
243 5th Avenue, Suite 136, New York, NY 10016

Copyright © 2018 by Cavendish Square Publishing, LLC

First Edition

No part of this publication may be reproduced, stored in a retrieval system, or transmitted in any form or by any means—electronic, mechanical, photocopying, recording, or otherwise—without the prior permission of the copyright owner. Request for permission should be addressed to Permissions, Cavendish Square Publishing, 243 5th Avenue, Suite 136, New York, NY 10016. Tel (877) 980-4450; fax (877) 980-4454.

Website: cavendishsq.com

This publication represents the opinions and views of the author based on his or her personal experience, knowledge, and research. The information in this book serves as a general guide only. The author and publisher have used their best efforts in preparing this book and disclaim liability rising directly or indirectly from the use and application of this book.

All websites were available and accurate when this book was sent to press.

Library of Congress Cataloging-in-Publication Data

Names: Miller, Derek L., author.
Title: Completing tasks : using algorithms / Derek Miller.
Description: New York : Cavendish Square Publishing, [2018] |
Series: Everyday coding | Includes bibliographical references and index. |
Identifiers: LCCN 2017022971 (print) | LCCN 2017024265 (ebook) |
ISBN 9781502629869 (E-book) | ISBN 9781502629838 (pbk.) |
ISBN 9781502629845 (6 pack) | ISBN 9781502629852 (library bound)
Subjects: LCSH: Computer algorithms--Juvenile literature.
Classification: LCC QA76.9.A43 (ebook) | LCC QA76.9.A43 M547 2018 (print) |
DDC 005.1--dc23
LC record available at https://lccn.loc.gov/2017022971

Editorial Director: David McNamara
Editor: Caitlyn Miller
Copy Editor: Nathan Heidelberger
Associate Art Director: Amy Greenan
Designer: Christina Shults
Production Coordinator: Karol Szymczuk
Photo Research: J8 Media

The photographs in this book are used by permission and through the courtesy of: Cover, Jonathan Kirn/The Image Bank/Getty Images; p. 4 granata68/Shutterstock.com; p. 8 omihay/Shutterstock.com; p. 10 adison pangchai/Shutterstock.com; p. 11 HO/AFP/Getty Images; p. 12 marekuliasz/Shutterstock.com; p. 13 Anna_Andre/Shutterstock.com; p. 14 Anastasiia Moiseieva/Shutterstock.com; p. 16 tacar/Shutterstock.com; p. 16, 27 wavebreakmedia/Shutterstock.com; p. 18 iris828/Shutterstock.com; p. 20 Roland Spiegler/Shutterstock.com; p. 21 Stilfehler/Wikimedia Commons/File:Traditional Addition Step 1.JPG; p. 22 Victority/Shutterstock.com; p. 25 Bushko Oleksandr/Shutterstock.com; p. 26 Yvonne Hemsey/Getty Images.

Printed in the United States of America

TABLE OF CONTENTS __

Coding with Algorithms

To achieve any goal, people follow steps. Whenever you tie your shoes, you complete a series of steps. If you do these steps correctly, you always end up with a knot. Computers are the same way. **Algorithms** are the steps that computers follow. Algorithms are sequences of instructions. When these instructions are performed, a **task** is completed. Algorithms

Opposite: An algorithm is a series of steps—just like tying your shoes!

can be very simple, such as 2 + 2. But they can also be very **complex**. Some of the most complicated computer **programs** in the world run on algorithms. They even play an important part in **artificial intelligence** and robotics.

There are many different **programming languages**. Different languages are used to perform different tasks. For example, some languages are used to make websites. Others make games. All these different programming languages are alike in some ways. They use many of the same tools to accomplish their goals. Algorithms are one of the most important tools they use.

Yet algorithms aren't just for computer programs. You can use them to describe tasks you do every day. Let's look at some examples.

CHAPTER 01

A Closer Look at Algorithms

Algorithms are like a recipe. A recipe tells us the order to add in ingredients. It is a list of steps to make food. An algorithm is also a list of steps. Algorithms are the backbone of many different computer programs. Sometimes, an algorithm's steps are very simple. Other times, they can be very complex. One simple algorithm finds the highest number in a group of numbers. It is very common in **computer programming**.

Computer games use algorithms to do all sorts of things. Minecraft uses them to create new worlds.

Imagine you are playing a computer game with some friends. When the match ends, the game needs to figure out who won. It can do this by looking at all the scores and finding the highest score. This is easy for us to do just by looking at the numbers. A computer needs to use an algorithm.

There is more than one algorithm to find the highest number. Most programming languages have a **command** to do it for you. Imagine you had to solve the problem. How would you do it? You might count up from one and cross out every number you counted until just one was left. This would leave you with the highest number. That's the winner. But what if the winning score was one hundred? It would be a long **process**!

The simplest way to find the winner is to compare two scores and cross out the lowest one. Just repeat this process until only one score is left. This is how computers find the highest number. It is a task that many games and programs do all the time. We don't even know it is happening behind the scenes. This

This is what computer code looks like. Algorithms are written in code.

algorithm is pretty simple. However, some are very complicated.

One example is Google's search algorithm. Every day, millions of people use it to find what they are looking for. The algorithm digs through over a billion websites. It ranks the best ones. Like all algorithms, Google's is based on three things. They are the **input**, the process, and the **output**.

The input is the starting data the algorithm uses. If you were making a recipe, it would be the ingredients you use. For Google, it is what you type into the **search bar**. This input is then put through the process to come up with the output. Here, the output is the search results that Google comes back with. In the recipe example, it would be the food you made. The process is where the

Google's website is very simple, but the algorithm it uses behind the scenes is incredibly complex.

steps of the algorithm take place. It is like putting your food in the oven. We know what happens to food when it cooks. But Google's process is a closely guarded secret. No one knows exactly what Google does with the input to search the internet for websites. If they did, they might start their own search engine website!

In computer programming, many things can be broken down to their input, process, and output—just as algorithms can be.

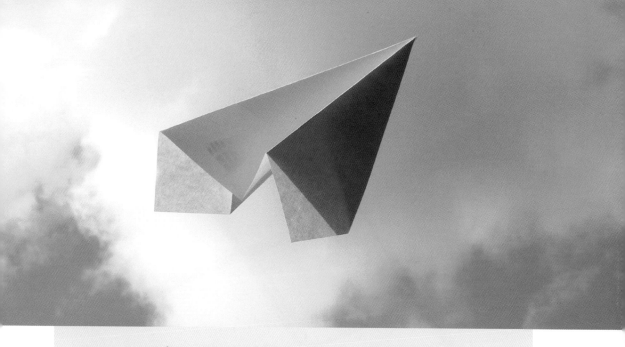

You can make a paper airplane many different ways. Each series of folds is like a different algorithm.

Algorithms in Flight

Can you think of an algorithm for making a paper airplane? What input do you need? What is your process to complete the task? If you did it correctly, your output should be able to fly through the air.

CHAPTER 02

Algorithms in Everyday Life

Every day, people complete many different tasks. Some are fun tasks, like solving a Rubik's cube. Often, tasks involve more than one step. These tasks can be written as algorithms. Take making a peanut butter and jelly sandwich as an example. The inputs are all the different

Opposite: Rubik's cubes look complicated, but anyone can solve them if they follow an algorithm.

The inputs are the ingredients on the left. The output is the finished sandwich on the right.

ingredients you need. The process is how you make it.

First, you spread jelly on one slice of bread. Then, you spread peanut butter on the other. Next, you put the two slices of bread together. The output is a finished sandwich.

This is a pretty simple task for us. It's also pretty easy for us to explain it to another person. But imagine trying to tell a robot how to do it. You would have to be really careful to tell it exactly what to do. You can't say "put the two slices of bread together" for the last step. A lot could go wrong. It might put the sandwich together so the jelly and peanut butter are on the outside. That would make a huge mess! People would use common sense. They know not to do this. Yet a computer always follows directions to the letter.

This can make computer programming quite tricky. You might think your directions make sense. Then, a computer follows them closely and does something silly. A person would just interpret what you said and do it right. However,

This girl completes a number of steps before she is ready to start art class.

a computer can't tell what you mean to say. It does exactly what you program it to do. This can create all sorts of **bugs** in computer programs.

Your daily routine is also like an algorithm. What do you do every morning before school? You wake up and get out of bed first. Then, you probably get dressed. Next, you might eat breakfast. Here, the order of some things isn't too important. Maybe you wear your pajamas to breakfast and change afterward. It doesn't really matter. Everyone has a slightly different algorithm for how they get ready in the morning. What's yours?

Algorithms also play an important part in mathematics. They are used to solve many

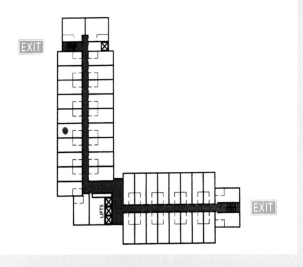

You use algorithms when you move around school.

Algorithms During the School Day

There are endless algorithms in daily life. If you complete a task by following a series of steps, you just used an algorithm. Can you think of any algorithms you use at school? For example, when it is time for PE, you use an algorithm to get from your classroom to the gym.

different sorts of problems. In fact, you already know some math algorithms. When you start to add two large numbers, you probably write them one on top of the other. Then, you add the ones, tens, and hundreds in order. After doing these steps, you have the correct answer. You've just used an algorithm to solve a math problem.

$$\begin{array}{r} 652 \\ +471 \\ \hline 3 \end{array}$$

This way of solving an addition problem is an algorithm.

CHAPTER 03

Bringing It All Together

Walking to a friend's house is an algorithm. You take a series of turns to get to the right house. Every time a person gets directions from his or her smartphone, it is the result of an algorithm. Many common tasks like this are powered by algorithms.

One fascinating way that algorithms are used is in the study of games. Did you know that it is

Opposite: An algorithm is what a smartphone uses to figure out the best way to get different places.

impossible to beat a computer at tic-tac-toe? The best you can do is tie. In fact, it is impossible to beat a skilled human player at tic-tac-toe. By following a few simple rules, a skilled player can never lose. This means tic-tac-toe is what we call a **solved game**. If you look at a game, you can always tell who will win, lose, or tie, unless one player makes a mistake.

A game like chess is not a solved game. It is a lot more complicated. It has a bigger board and more complex rules. This means that it is often unclear who will win. Both very skilled players and computers often cannot tell how the game will end. What you might not know is that checkers is now a solved game. There is a computer program that can never lose a game. At best, you can tie it. Actually, it is far more likely that the computer will

Algorithms tell a computer the best move to make in checkers.

win. It never makes a mistake. If you make even one mistake, it will beat you. Its success was made possible because of an algorithm.

The algorithm considers every possible move a player can make. Then, it looks at every possible move that could happen after that. Every turn further into the future it looks, it has to consider more and more possibilities. It examines many more possibilities than a person ever could. In the end, it picks the one that gives it the best chance of winning.

The supercomputer Deep Blue is famous for winning chess matches.

For checkers, the right algorithm guarantees that the computer will not lose. For a game like chess, it just makes it very unlikely. In this way, algorithms play a big role in artificial intelligence. When you play a game against a computer, it is likely using an algorithm.

Of course, games rely on a lot more than just algorithms. Many other tools are used. The more you learn about programming, the more interesting things you can do. If you start learning at a young age, you will be writing your own programs before you know it.

If it's rainy, you might take the bus to school.

Algorithms and Variables

Many algorithms use **variables**. Variables store information that can change. Algorithms can take these changes into account. Think about going to school. It's a series of steps that is like an algorithm. On a sunny day, you might ride your bike. If it is rainy, you might catch a ride. The weather is like a variable. Changes in the weather affect how you get to school.

GLOSSARY

algorithms Steps that computers follow to do something. Different algorithms do different jobs.

artificial intelligence The ability of some computers to "think" to complete tasks.

bugs Errors in computer programs.

command An order you can give a computer telling it to do something.

complex Not simple; complicated.

computer programming Creating a set of instructions so a computer does something.

input The starting data used by an algorithm or program.

output The end result of an algorithm or program.

process The steps an algorithm or program follows.

programming languages Languages used to make a computer program. You write code for different languages in different ways. Sometimes these are called coding languages.

programs Lists of instructions that a computer uses to do something.

search bar The box you type your search words into.

solved game A game that a computer can never lose.

task A job that a program can do.

variables Variables store information that can change. Variables let computer programs adapt to different circumstances.

FIND OUT MORE

Books

Gifford, Clive. *Awesome Algorithms and Creative Coding*.
New York: Crabtree Publishing Company, 2015.

Labrecque, Ellen. *Ada Lovelace and Computer
Algorithms*. North Mankato, MN: Cherry Lake
Publishing, 2017.

Websites

Coding: Algorithms

https://www.flocabulary.com/unit/coding-algorithms

Flocabulary presents a closer look at algorithms.

What Is an Algorithm?

http://www.bbc.co.uk/guides/zqrq7ty

Learn more about algorithms and how they are used.

INDEX

Derek Miller is a teacher who writes about history and technology. He is the author of *Information and Action: Using Variables* and *Group Planning, Creating, and Testing: Programming Together*. Derek likes to play chess against a computer program. Sometimes, he even wins.